DECLARATION OF THE RIGHTS OF GIRLS

First published in 2014 in French under the title *La déclaration des droits des filles* by Talents Hauts, France

This English edition first published in 2017 by

Little Island Books

7 Kenilworth Park

Dublin 6W, Ireland

First published in the USA in 2022

© Talents Hauts 2014

Translation © Little Island Books 2017

ISBN: 978-1-915071-20-0

A British Library Cataloguing in Publication record for this book is available from the British Library

Printed in Poland by L&C

Little Island receives financial assistance from The Arts Council/An Chomhairle Ealaíon

Little Island acknowledges the financial support of Literature Ireland for the translation of this book and for their ongoing support of translation in Ireland

This book is endorsed by Amnesty International Ireland (www.amnesty.ie)

10 9 8 7 6 5 4 3 2 1

Declaration of the Rights of Girls

Élisabeth Brami
Estelle Billon-Spagnol

Little Island

Girls have just as much right as boys to do the stuff they like. They have:

ARTICLE 1

The right to be untidy, scruffy, covered in scratches, hyper ...

Wheeeeee!

Heee

ARTICLE 2

The right to play marbles, play with cars,
rockets, train sets, and to play video games

ARTICLE 3

The right to be good at math and not so great at English

ARTICLE 4

The right to climb trees, build forts, scramble over fences ...

The right to wear sneakers,
hoodies, dungarees, shorts,
baseball caps ...

ARTICLE 6

The right to wear blue, black, khaki and all the colors of the rainbow

ARTICLE 7

The right to do any job they like:
truck driver, astronaut, police
chief, judge, factory manager,
president, sculptor, surgeon ...

ARTICLE 8

The right to learn judo, archery, boxing, football, fencing ...

ARTICLE 9

The right to read crime novels,
adventure stories, horror stories,
and to like scary movies

ARTICLE 10

The right to yell, stand up for themselves, fight, lose their temper, without being called a tomboy

ARTICLE 11

The right not to like sewing, knitting or tidying up

ARTICLE 12

The right to be disgusted when changing
a baby or wiping its nose

ARTICLE 13

The right to have really short hair

ARTICLE 14

The right not to be a princess every day

ARTICLE 15

The right to fall in love with anyone
they like: boy, girl or both

For Irena Milewska, a free woman – E. Brami

You will see the Amnesty logo on the cover of this book. That means that Amnesty International supports this 'declaration', which debunks received ideas and stereotypes – a quirky list of invented rights, which reminds us how important it is to value equality for all.

ARTICLE **15**

The right to fall in love with anyone they like: girl or boy or both

Alone at last!

For André Nahum, a free man – E. Brami

ARTICLE 14

The right not to be a superhero
every day

ARTICLE 13

The right to have long hair,
a pony tail, braids, dreadlocks ...

ARTICLE **12**

The right to wipe a baby's nose, change its diaper and look after it

The right to learn how to sew, to knit, to iron and to tidy up

The right to be a bit shy and scared,
not to like fighting and not to be muscly,
without being called a sissy

ARTICLE 9

The right to read love stories, poetry,
fairy tales, and the right to
cry at the movies

ARTICLE 8

The right to learn
ballet, flute or harp

ARTICLE 7

The right to do any job they like:
day-care-worker, school-teacher, dancer,
nurse, midwife, housekeeper ...

ARTICLE 6

The right to wear pink, yellow, purple and all the colors of the rainbow

WHEEE

ARTICLE 5

The right to be no good at DIY or hammering a nail and the right to hate getting their hands dirty

ARTICLE 3

The right to play with dolls,
at tea-parties, mommies-and-daddies,
skipping, hopscotch ...

ARTICLE 2

The right to be clean, sweet-smelling, stylish, cutesy, quiet and well-behaved – picture-perfect

me
me
me

NAH

I'm not crying

Muuum Muuuum
Mum Mum Mum
Mum

Not AGAIN?

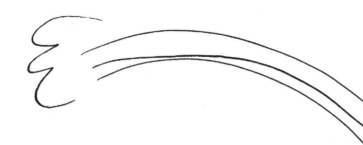

Boys have just as much right as girls to do the stuff they like. They have:

ARTICLE 1

The right to cry and to be hugged

Declaration of the Rights of Boys

Élisabeth Brami

Estelle Billon-Spagnol

Little Island

DECLARATION OF THE RIGHTS OF BOYS

First published in 2014 in French under the title *La déclaration des droits des garçons* by Talents Hauts, France

This English edition first published in 2017 by
Little Island Books
7 Kenilworth Park
Dublin 6W, Ireland

First published in the USA in 2022

© Talents Hauts 2014

Translation © Little Island Books 2017

ISBN: 978-1-915071-20-0

A British Library Cataloguing in Publication record for this book is available from the British Library

Printed in Poland by L&C

Little Island receives financial assistance from The Arts Council/An Chomhairle Ealaíon
Little Island acknowledges the financial support of Literature Ireland for the translation of this book and for their ongoing support of translation in Ireland

This book is endorsed by Amnesty International Ireland (www.amnesty.ie)

10 9 8 7 6 5 4 3 2 1